MLB's Greatest Teams

CHICAGO WHITE SOX

Dennis St. Sauver

Big Buddy Books
An Imprint of Abdo Publishing
abdobooks.com

abdobooks.com

Published by Abdo Publishing, a division of ABDO, PO Box 398166, Minneapolis, Minnesota 55439.
Copyright © 2019 by Abdo Consulting Group, Inc. International copyrights reserved in all countries. No part
of this book may be reproduced in any form without written permission from the publisher. Big Buddy Books™
is a trademark and logo of Abdo Publishing.

Printed in the United States of America, North Mankato, Minnesota.
102018
012019

THIS BOOK CONTAINS
RECYCLED MATERIALS

Cover Photo: Jamie Squire/Getty Images.
Interior Photos: 33ft/Depositphotos (p. 7); AP Images (pp. 15, 19, 22, 28); Brian Bahr/Getty Images (p. 23);
    Brian Kersey/Getty Images (p. 21); Daniel Bartel/AP Images (p. 5); Dylan Buell/Getty Images (p. 13);
    Everett Collection Inc/Alamy Stock Photo (p. 11); Jamie Schwaberow/Getty Images (pp. 24, 25); Jed
    Jacobsohn/Getty Images (p. 17); John Cordes/AP Images (p. 23); Jonathan Daniel/Getty Images (p. 9);
    Niday Picture Library/Alamy Stock Photo (p. 22); Ron Schwane/Getty Images (p. 27); Ronald Martinez/
    Getty Images (p. 29).

Coordinating Series Editor: Tamara L. Britton
Contributing Series Editor: Jill M. Roesler
Graphic Design: Jenny Christensen, Cody Laberda

Library of Congress Control Number: 2018948448

Publisher's Cataloging-in-Publication Data

Names: St. Sauver, Dennis, author.
Title: Chicago White Sox / by Dennis St. Sauver.
Description: Minneapolis, Minnesota : Abdo Publishing, 2019 | Series: MLB's
    greatest teams set 2 | Includes online resources and index.
Identifiers: ISBN 9781532118074 (lib. bdg.) | ISBN 9781532171116 (ebook)
Subjects: LCSH: Chicago White Sox (Baseball team)--Juvenile literature. |
    Baseball teams--United States--History--Juvenile literature. | Major League
    Baseball (Organization)--Juvenile literature. | Baseball--Juvenile literature.
Classification: DDC 796.35764--dc23

Contents

Major League Baseball

The Chicago White Sox is one of 30 Major League Baseball (MLB) teams. The team plays in the American League Central **Division**.

Throughout the season, all MLB teams play 162 games. The season begins in April and can continue until November.

4

The mascot for the White Sox is named Southpaw. He was born on the South Side of Chicago and he is left-handed. He became a green, furry fan favorite in 2004.

A Winning Team

The White Sox team is from Chicago, Illinois. The team's colors are black, silver, and white.

The team has had good seasons and bad. But time and again, the White Sox players have proven themselves. Let's see what makes the White Sox one of MLB's greatest teams!

Fast Facts

HOME FIELD: Guaranteed Rate Field

TEAM COLORS: Black, silver, and white

TEAM SONG: "Let's Go, Go-Go White Sox" by Captain Stubby and the Buccaneers

PENNANTS: 6

WORLD SERIES TITLES: 1906, 1917, 2005

CANADA

UNITED STATES
OF AMERICA

MEXICO

N
W E
S

Wisconsin

Iowa

LAKE MICHIGAN

Chicago

Illinois

Indiana

Missouri

Kentucky

Guaranteed Rate Field

The White Sox played in Comiskey Park for 81 years. The team moved to a new Comiskey Park stadium in 1991. This stadium became US Cellular Field in 2003. Its name changed again to Guaranteed Rate Field in 2016.

The field has a special Kids Zone. There, young fans can play **whiffle ball**, use batting and pitching cages, and learn base running skills.

The White Sox play against four other teams in the Central Division. They are the Cleveland Indians, Detroit Tigers, Minnesota Twins, and Kansas City Royals.

Then and Now

The team began playing as the White Stockings. In 1902, the name was shortened to the White Sox.

In 1919, eight team members were charged with taking money to lose in the World Series. This became known as the Black Sox **Scandal**. The players were banned from ever playing again.

The White Sox have been called the Cornhuskers, the White Stockings, the South Siders, and the ChiSox.

The White Sox lost the 1919 World Series. Over the next three decades, the team placed in the bottom three in its **division** 17 times.

So the team started **focusing** on speed and base running instead of home runs. The idea worked and the team earned the nickname Go-Go White Sox.

The White Sox are sometimes called the South Siders. The Chicago Cubs play on the other side of town.

Highlights

The Sox had its best seasons from 1951 to 1967. During this time, the team had 17 straight winning seasons. The Sox finished in second or higher in the Central **Division** six times.

Players won the division again in 1959. This time, they beat the feared New York Yankees.

In 1960, the Chicago White Sox became the first team to put players' last names on jerseys.

The top team from each AL and NL division goes to the playoffs. Each league also sends one wild-card team. One team from the AL and one from the NL will win the pennant. The two pennant winners then go to the World Series!

The White Sox had even more success during the 1990s and 2000s. The team had 12 winning seasons during that period. Players **celebrated** the success with a World Series victory in 2005.

The White Sox won the first four 2005 World
Series games against the Houston Astros.

Famous Managers

Al López was an MLB catcher before he **retired** in 1947. He was hired to manage the White Sox ten years later.

López managed the team from 1957 to 1965. And he came back in 1968 to manage for two more years. During this time, he also managed five AL All-Star teams. As the Sox's manager, López led the team to 11 straight winning seasons.

López joined the National Baseball Hall of Fame in 1977.

Ozzie Guillén played shortstop for the White Sox for 13 years. Six years later, he joined the team as its manager. He managed the Sox until 2011.

Guillén led the team to the 2005 World Series. There, he earned the 2005 Manager of the Year Award. In eight years, Guillén helped the Sox win 650 games!

Once he left the White Sox, Guillén went on to manage the Miami Marlins.

Star Players

Joe Jackson OUTFIELDER, #12

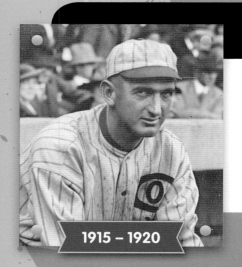

1915 – 1920

"Shoeless" Joe Jackson is one of the greatest ball players of all time. He was a great fielder and hitter. And he was fast! Shoeless Joe earned his nickname after he hit a **triple**. Then, he ran around the bases without his **cleats**! He hit nearly 80 triples in only six years with the Sox.

Luis Aparicio SHORTSTOP, #11

1956 – 1962
1968 – 1970

Luis Aparicio played shortstop for ten seasons with the Sox. He played more than 1,500 games during that time. Aparicio earned nine **Gold Glove Awards** for his skills as shortstop. He proved that speed and defense were important for winning. He was named to the National Baseball Hall of Fame in 1984.

Carlton Fisk CATCHER, #27

Carlton Fisk played in 1,236 games as catcher. He was named AL **Rookie** of the Year in 1972. He won the **Gold Glove Award** that same year. Fisk is second for the most home runs hit by a catcher. During his **career**, he hit more than 350 homers! He was **inducted** into the National Baseball Hall of Fame in 2000.

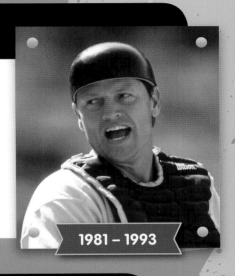

1981 – 1993

Frank Thomas FIRST BASEMAN, #35

1990 – 2005

Frank Thomas always wanted to play football. But he was a very talented baseball player. He hit 521 home runs during his career. And he hit more than 20 homers each season for eight years straight. Thomas earned the AL **Most Valuable Player (MVP)** Award in 1993 and 1994.

José Abreu FIRST BASEMAN, #79

2013 –

José Abreu was a star player in his home country of Cuba. He joined the Chicago White Sox in 2014. The Sox paid him $68 million for six years of play. Abreu earned a spot in the All-Star Game his first year. He was also named 2014 AL **Rookie** of the Year. He hit 36 homers that year. And he has hit more than 130 during his five-year **career**.

Avisail García RIGHTFIELDER, #26

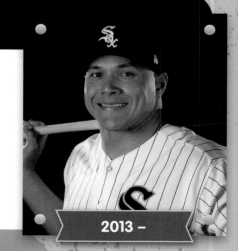

2013 –

Avisail García has been a great player since the Sox signed him in 2013. He had his best year in 2017. That year, he **putout** more than 260 batters. He also scored 75 runs and 18 homers. García made it onto the 2017 AL All-Star team. His excellent fielding and batting skills will help the team in the future.

Yolmer Sánchez SECOND BASEMAN, #5

Sánchez is the first player in MLB with the name Yolmer. He is very smooth with catching and throwing the ball. In 2017, he had many game-winning hits. Sánchez has **putout** more than 550 batters in only five seasons! He is one of the future stars of the Chicago White Sox.

2015 –

25

Final Call

The Chicago White Sox have a long, rich history. The team has played in five World Series, and earned three World Series titles.

Even during losing seasons, true fans have stuck by the players. Many believe the Chicago White Sox will remain one of the greatest teams in MLB.

Shortstop Tim Anderson *(left)* was second in the AL for most assists in 2018. He helped putout more than 340 batters during the season!

Through the Years

1901
The team moved to Chicago in 1900. Players took their first league title the next year.

1927
Comiskey Park had an upper deck added to the outfield. This new area could seat 23,200 more fans.

1955
The Sox scored an amazing 29 runs in a game against the Royals!

1976
Owner Bill Veeck tried to make the team more exciting. So he bought new uniforms that included shorts. The shorts were only worn three times.

28

1983

The team won the AL West **Division** title. This was the first time the Sox had been to the **playoffs** since 1959!

2000

The White Sox had one of its best teams since 1983. Many of the players were young stars.

2005

Jermaine Dye hit a **run batted in (RBI)** that allowed one runner to score. It was enough to win Game Four of the World Series. For this, Dye earned the World Series **MVP** Award.

2008

The White Sox paid players the fifth highest **salary** of all MLB teams.

Glossary

career a period of time spent in a certain job.

celebrate to observe a holiday or important occasion with special events.

cleats a strip fastened to the bottom of a shoe to prevent slipping.

division a number of teams grouped together in a sport for competitive purposes.

focus (FOH-kuhs) to give attention to.

Gold Glove Award annually given to the MLB players with the best fielding experience.

induct to officially introduce someone as a member.

Most Valuable Player (MVP) the player who contributes the most to his or her team's success.

playoffs a game or series of games to determine a championship or to break a tie.

30

putout an action that causes a batter or runner on the opposite team to be out.

retire to give up one's job.

rookie a player who is new to the major leagues until he meets certain criteria.

run batted in (RBI) a run that is scored as a result of a batter's hit, walk, or stolen base.

salary a fixed amount of money paid regularly for work done.

scandal something that angers or shocks people because rules or standards of behavior are violated.

triple a hit that lets the batter reach third base.

whiffle ball a plastic ball with holes in it.

Online Resources

Booklinks
NONFICTION NETWORK
FREE! ONLINE NONFICTION RESOURCES

To learn more about the Chicago White Sox, visit **abdobooklinks.com**. These links are routinely monitored and updated to provide the most current information available.

Index